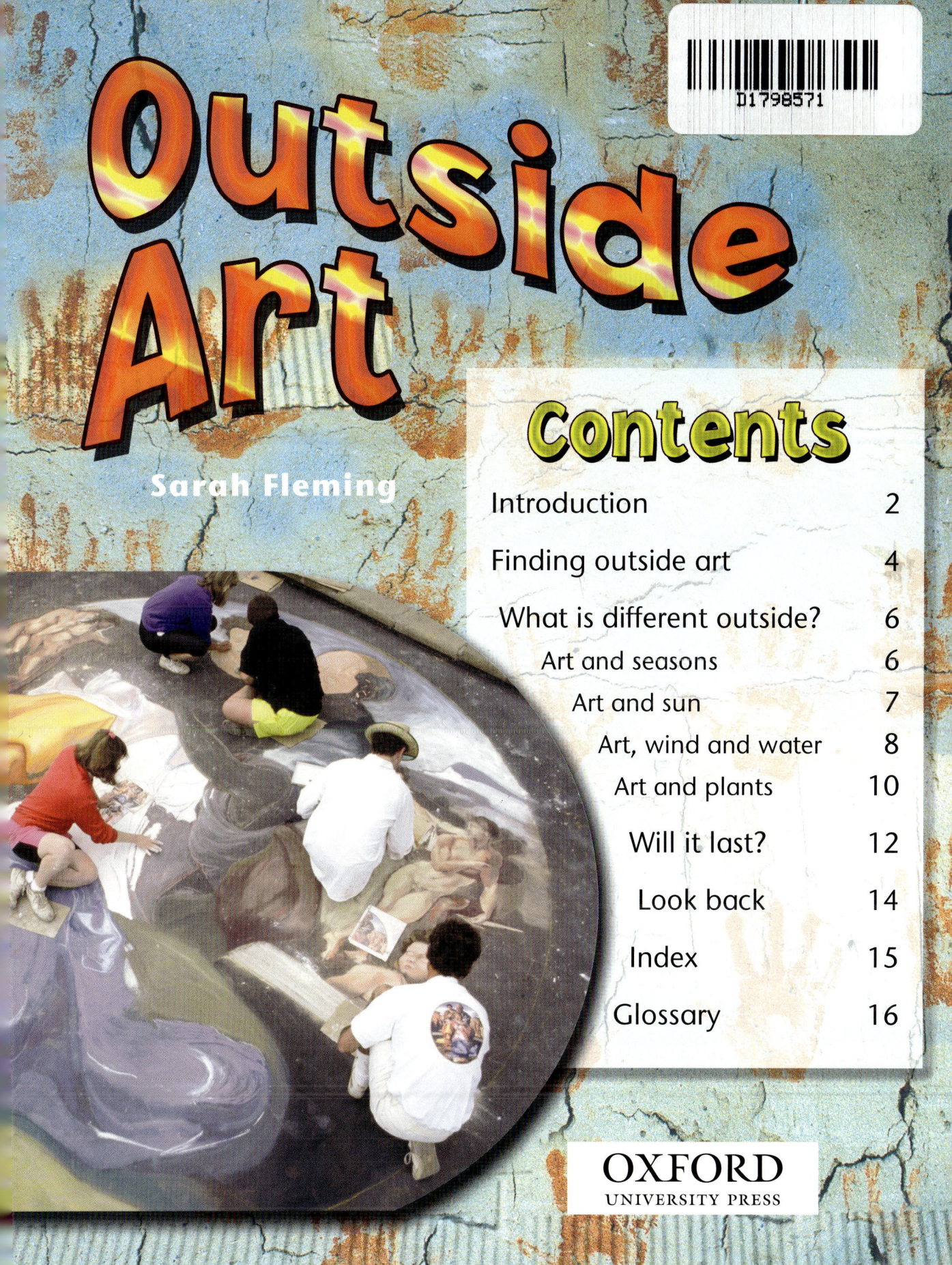

Outside Art

Sarah Fleming

Contents

OXFORD
UNIVERSITY PRESS

Introduction

There are many different sorts of outside art.

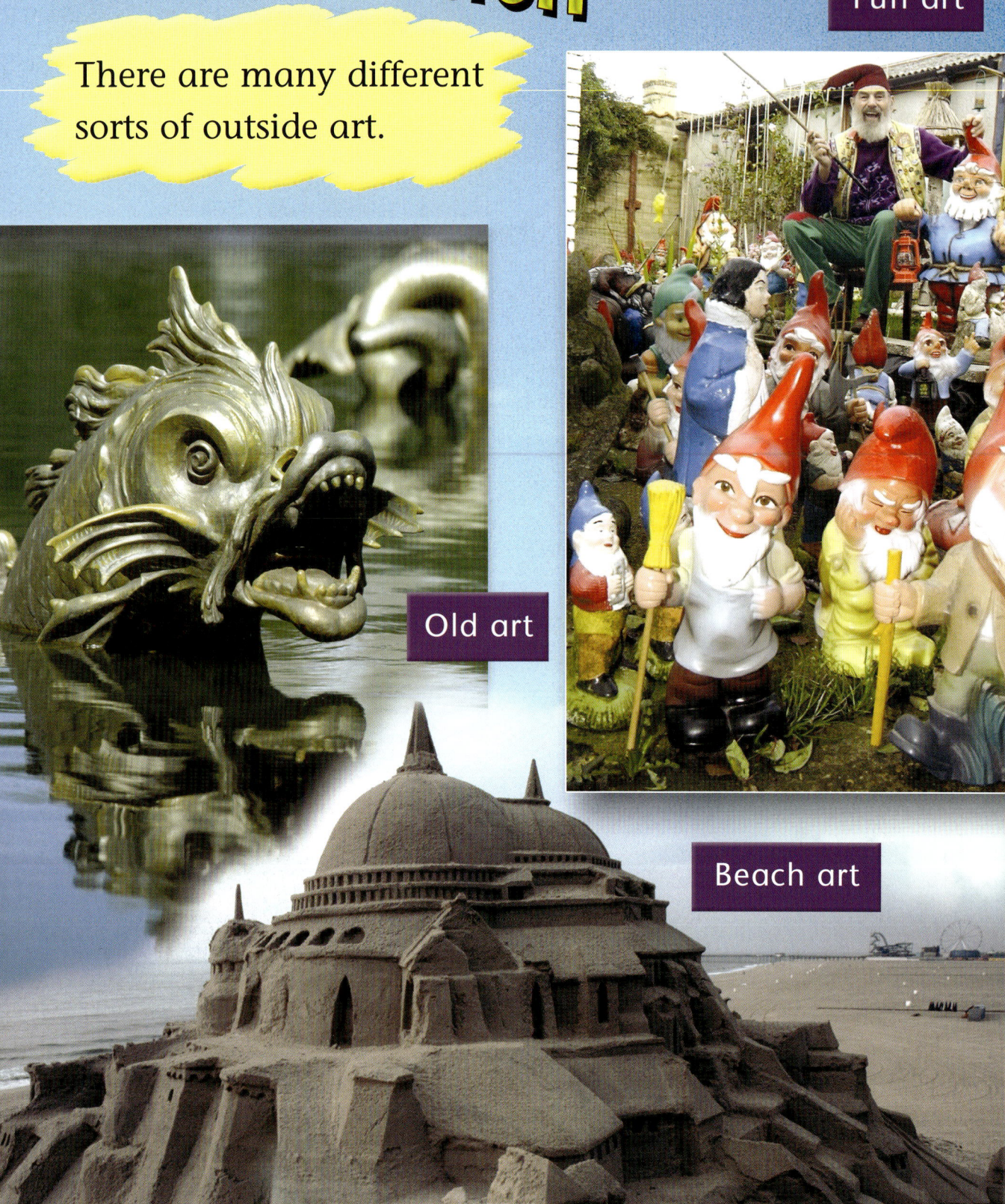

Fun art

Old art

Beach art

Park art

Wall art

Street art

You can make all sorts of outside things into art.

Finding outside art

You can find outside art in many different places.

You can find it in parks, gardens, woods and fields.

You can find it in streets and squares.

You can even find it in school grounds.

Is there outside art near where you live?

What is different Outside?

Many things make being outside different from being inside.

Seasons

Art and seasons

Outside art looks different in different seasons.

In which seasons were these photos taken?

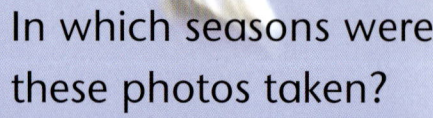

Art and sun

The light outside is from the sun.

The sun can shine through things.

The sun moves, so it makes different shadows through the day.

In Japan, people rake curves in gravel. These curves make shadows that change as the sun moves.

Art, wind and water

Wind can make art move. In the wind, art can make sounds too.

When the wind blows through a wind chime, the parts touch each other and make soft sounds.

Water can be a part of outside art.

Water can reflect things.

The painter, Monet, made this beautiful water garden. He painted this picture of it so people could enjoy it inside as well as outside!

Art and plants

You can use plants to make art.

Knot gardens are planted to grow into patterns.

Once a year, people in this town make a carpet of petals on the main street.

This body and face are made from plants and stone.

Plants can be grown and cut into shapes.

Flowers can be planted in models. This giant puppy bloomed into 70,000 flowers!

DEFINITION
Topiary (tope-ee-ary) – the art of cutting plants into shapes

11

Will it last?

Outside art does not last as long as inside art.

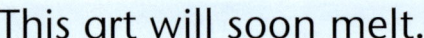
This art will soon melt.

Rain, wind and sun wear things away. This art will only last a few years.

This sand painting is made to bring rain. How long do you think it will last?

Art made out of stone lasts a long time, but it still wears away.

This is a detail from the sand painting. Can you find it in the main picture?

Art does not have to last for ever. The rain soon cleaned up this art!

Look back

1   Why does art made with plants have to be looked after?

2   How is light outside different from light inside?

3   Why does outside art wear away?

4   What can you use to make outside art?

5   What kinds of art could you put in your playground?

Index

Glossary

gravel little stones, used to cover ground

knot garden a garden planted with small hedges which make patterns

rake (noun) a garden tool with a comb-like end and a long handle

rake (verb) to move or shape something with a rake

seasons parts of the year that have different kinds of weather: spring, summer, autumn and winter

topiary the art of cutting plants into shape